WHAT IS A SOUTHLANDER?

WRITTEN BY
HELEN CAMPBELL
ILLUSTRATED BY
JAMES PATON

Oliver was a curious young rat who lived with his family behind a wall in a museum.

This was a wonderful home because there were great places to play hide and seek...

food scraps if you knew where to look...

...and no cats!

Rubbish

2

I t even had a classroom – for rats. As usual, Oliver was late for school. Down the stairs he zoomed...   over the large black cannon...

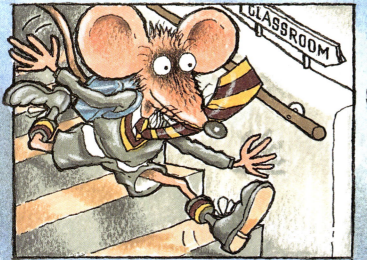

through the moa bones...   a quick swing on the ship's wheel...

and round past the old tuatara.

3

He made it just in time because he could hear those heavy footsteps – clomp, clomp, clomp.

In came their teacher Mr Esler, a giant rat with gentle eyes. He collected bones and knew lots about Southland. He loved taking the young rats on exciting trips to help them learn.

4

Today, Oliver raced home after school. "Mum, Dad!" he shouted, throwing his bag onto the floor. "Do YOU know what a Southlander is?"

"Mmmmmm," said his father thoughtfully, stroking his whiskers. "Is it a cheese?"

5

"No, no Dad," replied Oliver. "It's a person. Mr Esler said Southlanders are very special. They have big hearts, and you find them only in the best part of New Zealand."

"There are all kinds – big ones and little ones. Some become famous."

"They can live in the city or out in the country. Southland farmers give round things called swedes to their friends. They say words like GORRRE AND CHEERRRIO.

For holidays, lots of Southlanders stay in little houses called cribs...

and some go on adventures to places like Stewart Island."

"**S**outhlanders go to school just like us. When they grow up they find all sorts of jobs. They like helping each other."

"Sometimes they pack up their beds and go to places far far away like Dunedin, because they want to learn more."

"In winter, some Southlanders wear big shoes called gumboots.

They have Nanas or Grans who cook soup in large pots, and knit warm woolly jerseys."

9

"They eat strange food like muttonbirds (or titi), oysters, whitebait and toheroa."

"And cheese?" asked his father.

"Yes!" replied Oliver. "Mr Esler might take us to Edendale to nibble the cheese."
"I think I'll come too," murmured Dad.

CHEESE

"Their Mums and Dads take them to special places like...

Queen's Park

Oreti Beach

Splash Palace

the Water Tower..."

"And Edendale?" asked Dad, licking his lips.

"Southlanders like to have fun."

Netball

Rugby

Golf

Duck-shooting

Dancing

Singing

Skiing

Skateboarding

"Some climb very high mountains!"

12

"Dad, I WANT to be a Southlander," said Oliver, hopping up on to his father's knee.

"Well, let me see," said Dad, stroking his whiskers again.

"Do you live in Southland, Oliver?"
"YES, Dad."

"And do you eat cheese?"
"YES, Dad."

"Then... you ARE a Southlander," said his father. And he gave Oliver a great big rat hug.

P.S.
When you visit Southland's museum,
you might find a ship's wheel, the cannon,
a bear rug, Mr Esler, lots of bones,
and the old tuatara.

You will NOT find an Oliver...

This Book belongs to:

Arne Thynes

Some Special Southlanders I know:

I hope you
enjoy this book
Josephine

Hope to
see you
im NZ.
SAM

AUTOGRAPHS